Economics and Finance for Business

I0467881

Arthur H Tafero

Forward

This book is not for beginners. Beginning students and business people should examine my book, Introduction to Business – Second Edition, before attempting to tackle this more complex analysis.

This text is for business majors in college and experienced business people who wish to have a better understanding of how to compete for a position in the 8% of the population that is successful in business for three years or more.

There are extensive lesson plan outlines for both Finance and Macroeconomics (Bernanke) contained within this text. Finance is primarily concerned with larger public companies, and macroeconomics is primarily concerned with general knowledge of variables that can affect your business positively or negatively during the fiscal year.

Make sure you have mastered the principles of marketing and sales before attempting to understand these complex principles. In essence, finance is very simple; you borrow money for a business based on the expectation of sales in that business for the future. Most loans in this area are secured, which means that you will put up your house, retirement fund and other assets in order to finance your business.

The bank is not in the business of taking risks. They would much rather take your assets. Some banks live dangerously. They provide loans for businesses without 100% security; which is to say, they are gambling on your success. Sometimes banks like these go out of business themselves.

Since the odds of a business failing within three years are 92-8, it is highly advisable that you do not invest all of your assets into a business. (source: Wharton School of Business, Penn

University and Bank of China Small Loan Department, Beijing). Keep a portion of your savings and/or retirement funds safe for emergencies, just in case you become part of the 92% that fail.

If you are a banker or other professional business technician, it would behoove you to understand the principles of both finance and economics before making complex financial decisions.

Financing can be a useful, productive and profitable exercise, if practiced correctly. It can be a money pit for which you will have to pay for several years if you are not careful.

Economics and the variables contained in that discipline, hold the same promise for creating financial opportunities with patient understanding of the principles involved. Those who proceed without understanding these principles, move forward at their own risk, and are likely to become one of the 92%.

Arthur H Tafero

Table of Contents

Tafero's Lesson Plans of Day - Finance - An Overview of Finance - One

Lesson One – An Overview of Finance

Reference text for this lesson : Principles of Finance - Scott Besley, Eugene F. Brigham

Advisory* - The method of solving for any unknown in any economic or statistical formula contained in finance is as follows:

A. Carefully define and understand each of the variables within the formula
B. Formulae that include time variables assume that all other variables will be constant, which of course, is not possible.
C. Use a letter or symbol for each of the variables
D. Create a logical mathematical computation to achieve a result for the combining of the variables.

1. Financial markets 4 – banking in both domestic and international venues.
2. Investments 4 – security decisions of individuals and institutions.
3. Managerial finance 4 – banks and other institutions that choose securities for investment
4. Financial Implications 7 – There are financial implications in almost every business.
5. Causes of Globalization of Business 12 –
a. Improvements in transportation
b. Improvements in communication
c. Political shifts against protectionism
d. New technology
e. Outsourcing
Globalization has occurred naturally as a result of gradual evolution of international economies. Better transportation allows greatercommerce between countries and within each country. Better communication allows more financial transactions to occur within and outside of countries as well. The quality of these

4

transactions increases as the quality of the communication increases. While the recent global financial crisis has spurred a round of protectionism internationally, the general trend is still the lowering of protectionism in over 200 countries internationally. The lowering of this variable allows for greater trade volumes and more intercourse between countries. New technology allows countries to track their resources closer and save money on inventory expenses. Outsourcing allows countries to take advantage of lower wages for similar work in other countries and avoiding unnecessary labor costs in native countries where the cost of labor is far more expensive.

6. Financial Manager Responsibilities
Forecasting and Planning 14 – These are all educated guesses that provide a basis for a beginning Plan A that will evolve into a Plan B, according to the time-tested theory of the Chandler Strategy-Structure Relationship.
a. Major Investment and Financing Decisions 14 – Should a company seek to finance via long term debt? How about the interest costs for that strategy? Should a company finance via Stock? What if the stock is undervalued or overvalued?
b. Coordination and Control 14 – growth with efficiency
c. Financial Market Analysis 14 – money and capital markets, inflation, incentives

ICA 1 – HW 1

Write an essay on each of the following critical questions:

1. How has financing evolved since the 20th century?
2. Why should we study finance even if it is not our major?
3. How can you improve your personal financial decisions by studying finance?
4. Why is it likely the US will impose greater financial restrictions on financial markets and businesses after the global financial crisis?

Internet Resources for this lesson:

General Reference Material For All Content

http://www.askmrmovies.com

New Financial Restrictions in the US
www.demographia.com/db-overhang.pdf

IPOs

www.hoovers.com

Tafero's Lesson Plans of Day - Finance - Financial Assets - Two

Lesson Two – Financial Assets

1. Real Asset – 18 – A physically observable or touchable item
2. Financial Asset – 18 – A promise to distribute cash flow in the future
3. Treasury Bills -19 – Sold to countries or banks by the Treasury to finance governments
4. Repurchase Agreements – 19 – Banks selling investments with a repurchase promise
5. Federal Funds – 19 – Bank Reserve loans
6. Banker's Acceptance – 19 – Company promise to pay
7. Commericial Paper –19 - Loan issued by strong companies
8. Negotiable CDs – 19-Bank Interest
9. Eurodollars – 19- Dollar deposits in Europe
10. Money Market Funds – 19 – Investments in T-Bills, CDs and other short-terms
11. Municipal Bonds – 19 – Issued by states and cities
12. Term Loans – 19 – Loans over specified periods
13. Mortgages – 19 – house loans
14. Corporate Bonds -19 – company shares less risky than stocks
15. Preferred Stock – 19 – company stock less risky than common shares
16. Common Stock – 19 – risky shares of stock
17. Common Equity 20 – part of company owned by the public
18. Par Value – 21 – face value of a stock
19. Retained Earnings – 21- Earnings not paid out to shareholders
20. Additional Paid-In Captial – 21 – Difference between new stock issue and par value

21. Maturity Value – 22 – The value of a debt a lender receives at the end of the loan

22. Interest Payments -22- Payments made for debt

23. Maturity Date – 22 – The last day you can pay principal debt with additional interest

24. Call Provision – 29 – A corporation's right to pay bonds before maturity

25. Sinking Fund – 29 – A set payment each month to lower bond repayments

26. Convertible Features – 30 – A shareholder's right to convert bonds into stocks

27. *Bond Ratings – 31 – guesses as to the actual worth of company bonds. Numerous AAA rated bonds went bankrupt during the last global financial crisis irrefutably proving that ALL bond ratings are merely educated guesses. (see lesson on Bond Ratings)

28. Risk Free Bonds – 32 – AAA bonds rated risk-free, such as AIG, Morgan-Stanley, Merril Lynch and others all went bankrupt, indicating there really is no such thing as a risk-free bond. Financial analysts GUESS that these bonds are AAA and risk-free, but that does not necessarily make them so.

29. Downgrading – 33 – The lowering of a bond rating by an established investment company such as Standard and Poors (which admittedly makes numerous mistakes in both directions of rating; Some Asian investment analyst companies have now ignored Western ratings and rate company bonds based on their own criteria.

30. *Derrivatives – 39 – Financial assets that have value from other assets such as stocks and bonds. This is actually valuing an item not based on what it is actually worth, but what it MIGHT be worth factoring in stocks and bonds. The problem of this calculation is that the stocks and bonds used in recalculating the new worth may be wildly overvalued (such as the hundreds ofstocks and bonds of companies that went under during the global financial crisis). If thosestocks and bonds are unrealistic representations of these assets, then the asset itself becomes highly unreliable as a calculated item and the derivative from this asset is merely a WILD guess, usually far too high on the upside. (See Lesson on Bond Ratings)

31. *Hedge Funds – 40 – Hedge funds are options to buy or sell

an asset at a predetermined price. It is similar to a put and call process in the stock market. In simple terms you PUT in an order to buy if a stock hits $30 a share. If the shares fall to $20 a share you make a CALL to sell your shares. In Hedge Funds, instead of buying a stock at $30 with a PUT, you sell it (after you have bought it at $20 a share), but you still retain the right to sell it if it goes back down to $20. (See Lesson on Bond Ratings)
32. Risk and Return – 43 – See chart on page 43. The greater the risk of a security, the greater the return (or loss).

ICA 2 – HW 2

1. Discuss the advantages and disadvantages of debt and preferred stock from an issuer's standpoint.
2. Discuss the advantages and disadvantages of debt and preferred stock from an investor's standpoint.
3. How are convertible securities used to help firms raise funds?
4. What are the advantages and disadvantages of common stock financing?

Internet Resources for this lesson:

General Reference Material For All Content

http://www.askmrmovies.com

Stocks

www.money.msn.com/business-news/news.aspx

Bonds

www.bloomberg.com/news/bonds/

Tafero's Lesson Plans of Day - Finance - Financial Markets - Three

LESSON 3 – Financial Markets and the Investment Banking Process

1. Financial Markets - 82 – Individuals and organizations that bring together borrowers and savers
2. Money Markets – 82 – short-term financial assets
3. Capital Markets – 82 – long-term financial assets
4. Debt Markets – 82 – bonds and other loans such as mortgages
5. Equity Markets – 82 – stocks and trading
6. Primary Markets – 82 – countries or states issuing bonds
7. Secondary Markets – 82 – trading in previously issued securities
8. Stock Market – 82 – institution that reports stock prices
9. Listing Requirements – 82 – standards required for someone or some company to trade on a local or regional stock exchange
10. Investment Bankers – 82 – individuals who help to set the price for IPOs
11. SEC (Securities and Exchange Commission – 82 – agency established to protect the investor from fraud
12. International Financial Markets – 82 – Market share of world equities has increased while investment in US markets have decreased.
13. IPO (Initial Public Offering) – 82 – small company's first entry into the stock market.

ICA and HW 3

Write an essay on each of these questions:

1. How does an efficient capital market help to reduce the prices of goods and services?
2. Why would a company be interested in getting a wide distribution of its shares?

3. Why do you think some companies prefer to be listed on the NYSE instead of their own country's stock exchange?
4. What types of companies enter the market for IPOs (Initial Public Offerings)?

Internet Resources for this lesson:

General Reference Material For All Content

http://www.askmrmovies..com

Stock Exchanges

www.tdd.lt/slnews/Stock_Exchanges/Stock.Exchanges.html

Debt Markets

www.investorwords.com/1322/debt_market.html

Tafero's Lesson Plans of Day - Finance - Financial Intermediaries - Four

Lesson 4 – Financial Intermediaries

1. Financial Intermediaries – 117 – transfer funds by issuing their own securities and purchasing the securities of others. Also known as the secondary market, it was one of the areas that created the last Global Financial Crisis when some insurance companies such as AGI began to buy thousands of toxic loans that were almost guaranteed to default.
2. Economic Efficiency – 117 – making the most transactions for the most money in the least amount of time with the least amount of work. Economic reforms that are too efficient, however, sometimes have the adverse effect of allowing fraud to more easily prevail in lax banking situations.
3. Diversification – 117 – Having a range of investments instead of investing all funds in area.
4. Commercial Banks – 117 – Major lenders to businesses. Commercial Banks were a large part of the Global Financial Crisisbecause they were making loans based on unrealistic estimates of assets of companies that overstated their net worth by as much as 100X of their true value.
5. Credit Unions – 117 – Major lenders to consumers. Most of these banks did not suffer as badly as the commercial banks during the Global Financial Crisis. Most personal loans were still eventually repaid unless the individual declared bankruptcy.
6. Thrift Institutions – 117 – Major lenders to house buyer with mortgages. These banking institutions were slaughtered during the recent Global Financial Crisis because they made large loans on houses that were not really worth even half of the money that was being loaned. When the mortgage holders could not repay the loan,the banks foreclosed on the houses to get their loans back, but the houses were now only worth half as much. For example, if a bank gave a $200,000 mortgage loan on a house the owner paid $20,000 down and $1000 a month for a mortgage, they might not be able to pay the mortgage after three years. Now they have given the bank $36,000 plus the $20,000

down payment for total payments of $56,000. But after the Global Financial Crisis, the house is now only worth $100,000 and the bank, even it forecloses, can only get $156,000 back for it $200,000 loan minus the expenses of selling the house again. These are part of what is known as toxic loans.

7. Federal Reserve System – 117 – Central Bank of the United States which manages the money supply and the stability of state banks.

8. Banking Legislation – 117 – Has seen periods of tight restrictions such as after the Great Depression and periods of loose restriction; the period until the Global Financial Crisis. Now the trend is to tighten restrictions similar to the period after the Great Depression.

ICA 4 – HW 4

Write an essay on each of these questions:

1. Why are financial intermediaries useful?
2. Why must banks maintain the confidence of the public?
3. Why is deregulation of banks dangerous for consumers?
4. How do US banks differ from banks in other countries?

Internet Resources for this lesson:

General Reference Material For All Content

http://www.askmrmovies.com

Runs on Banks
www.investopedia.com

Deregulation of Banks
www.ehow.com

Tafero's Lesson Plans of Day - Finance - The Cost of Money (Interest) - Five

Lesson Five – The Cost of Money (Interest)

A depiction of the first tightening of lending regulations

1. Dollar Return – 139 – income paid by the issuer or the change in value of a financial asset in the financial market
2. Interest – 139 – price of renting money.
3. Cost of Money Factors (Interest) – 139
a. Production opportunities
b. Time preferences for consumption
c. Risk
d. Inflation
These four variables are calculated to create an interest rate

4. Term Structure of Interest Rates – 139 – the relationship between the yields on securities and the securities' maturities.
5. Yield Curve – 139 – an indicator that uses variables such as demand for short-term funds and inflation.
6. Interest Rate Effect – 139 – Interest rates affect stock market prices. Higher interest rates slow down growth and stock priceincreases.
7. Liquidity Preference Theory – 135 – long term bonds normally have higher yields than short-term bonds.
8. Market Segmentation Theory – 135 – Each lender and borrower has a preferred maturity. Some clients prefer short term loans and other prefer to have a longer repayment period.
9. Expectations Theory – 134 – Professional guess about the yield curve based on future inflation rates
10. Inflation Premium – 129 – a surcharge in the interest rate based on a professional guess that inflation will erode the investment. It must be noted that there is seldom a Deflation Discount or lowering of the interest rate based on a professional guess that deflation will increase the value of an investment.

ICA and HW 5

Write the following Essay Questions:

1. How do interest rates affect the Stock Market?
2. How do interest rates affect the Real Estate Market?
3. Why are all yields merely professional guesses?
4. In your opinion, do interest rates affect the stock market or does the performance of the stock market affect interest rates. Why?

Internet Resources for this lesson:

General Reference Material For All Content

http://www.askmrmovies.com

Interest Rates

www.stockcharts.com/charts/YieldCurve.html

Yields

www.investopedia.com

Tafero's Lesson Plans of Day - Finance - Business Organizations and Taxes

Lesson 6 – Business Organizations and the Tax Environment -6

Small Business Owners' View of IRS

1. Proprietorship 149 – an unincorporated business owned by oneindividual
Advantages:
a. Easily formed
b. Inexpensive
c. Few government regulations
d. Taxed as an individual, not as a corporation

Disadvantages:
a. Unlimited personal liability
b. Difficulty obtaining capital
c. Difficulty in transferring ownership
d. Limited to the life of the individual

2. Partnership 150 – same as a proprietorship except it has two or more owners
Advantages:
a. Easily formed
b. Inexpensive
c. Few government regulations
d. Individually taxed, not as a corporation
Disadvantages:
a. Unlimited liability for the owners
b. Limited life for the company
c. Difficulty of transferring ownership
d. Difficulty in raising large amounts of capital

3. Corporation 151 – A corporation is a legal entity created by a state. It is separate and distinct from its owners and managers. Advantages:

a. A corporation can continue after it original owners and managers die, so it has unlimited life.

b. Ownership interests can be divided into shares of stock and those shares can be transferred.

c. There is limited liability in corporations. Your liability is strictly limited to your investment.

Disadvantages:

a. Corporate earnings are subject to double taxation. Corporation is taxed and then individualearnings are taxed.

b. Paperwork and maintenance is far more difficult than proprietorships or partnerships.

4. Corporate Charter – 151 – includes name of corporation, types of activities, amount of capital stock, number of directors, and names and addresses of the directors.

5. Hostile Takeovers – 158 – companies with undervalued stocks bought by another company.

6. Poison Pill – 158 – methods used by companies facing hostile takeovers to avert a hostile takeover.

7. Greenmail – 159 – paying a high premium for stock acquired by a potential takeover agent

8. Stakeholders – 160 – employees, customers, suppliers and shareholders.

9. External Environment – 161 – Factors outside the company that affect Stock Price

a. Laws

b. Environment

c. Federal Reserve

d. International economies

e. National economy

10. External Factor Evaluation (EFE) – a mathematical evaluation of the external factors.

11. Business Ethics – a mostly imaginary code of conduct for businessmen. Most ethics in business are secondary to profits.

12. Multinational Corporations

a. Enter new markets

b. Obtain additional raw materials

c. Discover new technologies

d. Improve efficiency

e. Avoid political problems

Problems of Multinationals

a. Currency exchange

b. Foreign laws

c. Language problems

d. Cultural differences

e. Government interference

13. Capital Gains versus Ordinary Income 170 – Ordinary income is usually a salary. Capital gains is a profit realized on capital invested over the period of one tax year. If you buy a stock for 20 and it goes to 40, you must pay X amount of dollars in tax for your net profit.

14. Corporate Taxes – 172 – It is much easier to avoid paying taxes in a corporation than fromordinary income. There are a vast number of deductions for businesses that are not allowed for individuals.

ICA and HW 6

Write an essay for these questions:

1. How do proprietorships, partnerships and corporations differ?

2. How do taxes differ from wage earners to people who invest in stocks?

3. How can you sometimes prevent a hostile takeover?

4. How do Multinational companies differ from domestic companies?

Internet Resources for this lesson:

General Reference Material For All Content

http://www.askmrmovies.com

Mulitnationals

www.investopedia.com

Tax Structure of the US

www.mitpress.mit.edu/catalog/item/default.asp?ttype=2&tid

Tafero's Lesson Plans of Day - Finance - Financial Statements - Seven

Lesson 7 – Financial Statements

1. Income Statement – 189 – a document that shows profits and losses issued anywhere from once a month to once year, but most commonly every quarter.
2. The Balance Sheet – 190 – a document that shows the financial position of a company at a specific moment in time.
3. Statement of Retained Earnings – 193 – a document that shows a claim against assets. The higher or lower the retained earnings, the higher or lower the dividends paid to stockholders.
4. Statement of Cash Flow – 195 – This document exclusively analyzes where the cash came from and where it went.
5. Liquid Asset – 199 – an asset that can easily be converted to cash without significant loss.
6. Liquidity Ratios – 199 – a document that shows how much of a company's assets are liquid in comparison to its total assets.
7. Acid Test – 201 = Current Assets – Inventories/Current Liabilities
8. Fixed Assets Turnover Ratio – 203 = Sales/Net Fixed Assets
9. Total Assets Turnover Ratio – 204 = Sales/Total Assets
10. Financial Leverage – 204 – An unhealthy business practice of taking unnecessary loans in order to reduce the amount paid to stockholders as dividends. This is done because dividends are taxable and interest on loan is not. This is a classic short-termsolution to a long-term problem that often ends up in chaos.
11. Debt Ratio – 205 – Another unhealthy number if it is too high. This document measures Total Debt/Total Assets. Low ratios are healthy companies and high ratios are companies living on the edge.
12. Times Interest Earned (TIE) ratio 206 = Earnings Before

Interest and Taxes (EBIT)/Interest Charges

13. Profitability Ratios – 207 = Net Profit Margin (profit per dollar of sales) = Net Income/Sales

14. Return on Total Assets – 208 = Net Income/Total Assets

15. Return on Common Equity – 208 = Net Income to Common Stockholders/Common Equity of Stockholders

16. Price/Earnings (PE) Ratio – 209 - Earnings Per Share = Net Income to Stockholders/Number of Shares of Common Stock

17. Book Value Per Share – 209 – Total Common Share Ownership/number of shares outstanding

18. Market/Book Ratio – 210 – Market Price per share/Book Value per share.

19. Trend Analysis – 211 – a valuable measuring tool in graph form that shows your company performance in relation to the rest of the industry (or the pie).

ICA and HW 7

Answer these essay questions:

1. How does a balance sheet give us a picture of a company?
2. How does a cash flow statement give us a picture of how cash is used in a company?
3. Why are liquid assets important to a company?
4. Why should you know the debt ratio of a company before investing in it?

Internet Resources for this lesson:

General Reference Material For All Content

http://www.askmrmovies.com

Balance Sheets

www.investopedia.com

Quarterly Reports

www.investorwords.com/4004/quarterly_report.html

Tafero's Lesson Plans of Day - Finance - Financial Planning and Control - Eight

Lesson 8 – Financial Planning and Control

1. R&D should be the most important part of any financial projection or guess. Exhaustive research should be performed before Plan A is put into effect. And even despite this research, Plan A will fail at some point and the new Plan B will have to make adjustments for the miscalculations of Plan A. (not in book)

2. All forecasting and plans are nothing more than professional guesses. No one can see the future for even one day, although some unethical financial planners like to give the impression that their numbers are foolproof or almost foolproof. I would put the emphasis on the proof, and not the fool who projects them as foolproof. (not in book)

3. Breakeven Analysis – 245 – the point where sales will cover operating expenses.

4. Financial Leverage – 254 – increases or decreases in net profit affects future plans.

5. Cash Budgeting – 259 – Monthly budgets designed to monitorcash flow and expenses.

6. Financial Planning 265 – projections (guesses) of sales, incomesand assets as well as liabilities

7. Financial Control – 265 – Method of initiating Plan B when Plan A inevitably needs modification.

8. Operating Leverage – 266 – the extent of fixed costs within a firm's operation.

9. Degree of Operating Leverage (DOL) – 266 – indicates how a change in sales will affect operating income

10. Degree of Financial Leverage – 266 – shows how a change in EBIT will affect EPS.

11. Total Leverage – 266 – extent to which total fixed costs

(operating and financial) exist in a firm's operation.
12. Degree of Total Leverage (DTL) – 266 – shows how increases or decreases in sales will effect the EPS.

ICA and HW 8

Write an essay for each of these questions:

1. Explain how profits or losses will be magnified for a firm with a high operating leverage.
2. Explain how profits or losses will be magnified for a firm with a high financial leverage.
3. How would the breakeven point be affected by these four variables?
a. Increase in sales price
b. Reduction in labor costs
c. Issuing new bonds
d. Decrease in fixed operating costs
4. Why should cash budgets be created?

Internet Resources for this lesson:

General Reference Material For All Content

http://www.askmrmovies.com

Operating Leverage

www.accountingformanagement.com/operating_leverage.htm

Financial Leverage

www.investopedia.com

Tafero's Lesson Plans of Day - Finance - Valuation - Nine

Lesson 9 – Valuation Concepts

1. Basic Valuation – 340 – is based on the present value of the cash flows that the asset is expected to produce in the future.
2. Bond Valuation – 341 – a bond's market price is determined by the cash flows that it generates.
3. Model – 342 – an equation or set of equations designed to show how one or more variables affect some other variables. All models are subject to limitations of time, which is to say, they are guesses about the future based on X number of variables for X length of time.
4. Interest Yield – 347 – also known as the current yield, it is the interest paid on a bond
5. Capital Gains Yield – 347 – the percentage gain or loss in the value of an investment. For example, a mortgage on a house bought for $100,000 after the Global Financial Crisis might still be $50,000 if you paid off half of the mortgage, but if the house is now valued at $70,000, you would be taking a capital gains loss on your investment if you sold it for $70,000.
6. Discount Bond – 349 – a bond that sells below its par value when the interest rates rise.
7. Premium Bond – 349 – a bond that sells above its par value when the interest rates fall.
8. Yield to Maturity – 349 – the average rate of return earned on a bond if it is held to maturity.
9. Interest Rate Price Risk – 353 – the risk of changes in bond prices when interest rates change
10. Interest Reinvestment Rate Risk – 354 – the risk that income from a bond will vary when it we reinvest in it when the interest rateschange.
11. Market Price – 358 – price at which a stock sells in the stock market.
12. Intrinsic Value – 358 – the actual value of a stock in the stock market based on its balance sheet valuation.

13. Growth rate – 358 – the expected (guess) of change in dividends per share of stock. This can be negative as well.
14. Required Rate of return - 359 – what a buyer expects to get from a stock; this is another guess.
15. Capital Gains Yield – 359 – The increase or loss of a stock over the course of one year. There are various questionable models that plug in a value for each of the variables involved, but both the variables and the passage of time are so uncertain as to render ANY of these economic models no more than an educated guess. Since investments are over various periods of time, ALL of them are purely GUESSES (because no one can foresee the future for even one day).

ICA and HW 9

If your stock falls from $50 to $5, do you
really think your stock options are valuable?

Write an essay for each of these questions:

1. How do you determine the value of an asset?
2. How do you evaluate a stock before purchasing it?
3. How do real asset valuations differ from financial assets?
4. Why are all economic models and formulae that include time merely guesses?

Internet Resources for this lesson:

General Reference Material For All Content

http://www.askmrmovies.com

Certainty of Failure of Plan A (All Economic Models)

http://www.factoidz.com – Tafero Certainty of Failure of Plan A

Economic Models

www.econmodel.com/classic

Tafero's Lesson Plans of Day - Finance - Risk and Rate of Return - Ten

Lesson 10 – Risk and Rates of Return

1. Risk – 384 - the chance an outcome other than the expected one will occur
2. Probability – 385 - chance that the event will occur. This is based on an educated guess and the longer in the future the guess is for the more likely the guess will be grossly inaccurate.
3. Expected Rate of Return – 387 – this is the weighted average of the outcomes base on probability. These educated guesses are more likely to be inaccurate the longer in the future they are predicted.
4. Discrete Probability Distribution – 388 – The number of possibleoutcomes is limited or finite. This allows for a more accurate outcome than a guess that has infinite possibilities.
5. Continuous Probability Distribution – 388 – the number of possibleoutcomes is infinite, therefore the probability of an accurate outcome from an educated guess is far less likely than a discrete probability distribution.
6. Standard Deviation – 389 – a statistical variable that measures the tightness or variability of a set of outcomes. When the SD is small, the outcome is more likely, when it is large, the outcomes are more uncertain.
7. Risk aversion – 394 – seeking lower risk in exchange for lower returns
8. Risk premium – 394 – receiving higher returns for taking greater risks
9. Portfolio risk – 395 – ideally, a portfolio should be matched to the age and needs of the investor. Younger investors can take more risk and older investors seek lower risk.
10. Expected Return – 396 – an educated guess on what you should gain from a stock.
11. Realized Rate of Return – 396 – the actual numbers of your return, which are different from the educated guesses well over 50% of the time. Sometimes the actual numbers differ as much as over 90% of the time in down markets.
12. Firm-Specific Risk – 402 – investing in only one stock

13. Market Risk – 402 – External Factors that affect all investments (global financial crisis)

ICA and HW 10

Answer these essay questions:

1. How are expected rate of return and required rate of return on a stock different?
2. How much credence should you give probability calculations to the evaluation of the anticipated increase of a stock?
3. How should we assess risk?
4. Why should we have a balanced portfolio?

Internet Resources for this lesson:

General Reference Material For All Content

http://www.askmrmovies.com

Risk

www.investorguide.com/igu-article-823-stock-basics-measuring-a-stock&rsq...

Balanced Portfolio

www.beginnersinvest.about.com/od/assetallocation1/.../aa102404.htm

Tafero's Lesson Plans of Day - Finance - Cost of Capital - Eleven

Lesson 11 – The Cost of Capital

Money costs money

Advisory* - The method of solving for any unknown in any economic or statistical formula contained in finance is as follows:

E. Carefully define and understand each of the variables within the formula
F. Formulae that include time variables assume that all other variables will be constant, which of course, is not possible.
G. Use a letter or symbol for each of the variables
H. Create a logical mathematical computation to achieve a result for the combining of the variables.

1. Kd 435= the interest rate on the firm's debt stated on a before-tax basis
2. KdT 435= the after-tax component cost of debt, where T is the firm's marginal tax rate
3. Kps 435 = the component cost of preferred stock.
4. Ks 435 = the component cost of retained earnings.
5. Capital Structure – 436 – The combination or mix of different types of capital used by a company
6. After-Tax Cost of Debt (KdT) – 437 – The cost of new debt less the deductibility of tax that is used to calculate the weighted average cost of capital. (WACC)

7. Cost of Preferred Stock (Kps) – 438 – the rate of return that investors require on the firm's preferred stock.

8. Cost of Retained Earnings (Ks) – 439 – Rate of return required by stockholders on the earnings that are retained by the company for reinvestment.

9. Flotation – 443 – the expenses incurred when issuing new securities.

10. Marginal Cost of Capital – 446 – the cost of obtaining one dollar of new capital using a weighted average

11. Marginal Cost of Capital Schedule – 446 – A graph that shows the firm's weighted average cost of each new dollar of capital raised.

12. Break Point – 449 – the dollar value of new capital that can be raised before an increase in the company's weighted average cost of capital occurs.

ICA and HW 11

Answer these essay questions:

1. How would a lower corporate tax rate affect Kdt, Ks and WACC?

2. How would a company increasing its dividend payout ratio affect Kdt, Ks and WACC?

3. How would expansion of the company into a risky new area affect Kdt, Ks and WACC?

4. How would a more conservative investor base in a company affect Kdt, Ks and WACC?

Internet Resources for this lesson:

General Reference Material For All Content

http://www.askmrmovies.com

KdT
www.financial-dictionary.thefreedictionary.com/Cost+of+Debt

WACC
www.investopedia.com/terms/w/wacc.asp

Tafero's Lesson Plans - Finance - Capital Budgeting - Twelve

Lesson 12 – Capital Budgeting

How much of the pie will you get?

1. Capital Budgeting – 474 – The process of planning expendituresof assets whose cash flow are expected to extend beyond one year.

2. Replacement Decisions – 475 – decisions about whether to purchase capital assets (also known as fixed assets) to maintain production.

3. Expansion Decisions – 475 – decisions about whether to purchase capital assets and add them to existing assets.

4. Independent Projects – 475 – projects whose cash flows are not affected by the acceptance of other projects.

5. Mutually Exclusive Projects – 476 – A set of projects where the acceptance of one project means that the other projects cannot be accepted.

6. Cash Flows – 477 – Actual cash, as opposed to accounting profits that a company receives or pays during a specific period.

7. Incremental Cash Flow – 478 – The change in a company's net cash flow resulting from an investment project.

8. Sunk Cost – 479 – Cash outlay that has already been spent and that cannot be recovered.

9. Opportunity Cost – 479 – The return on the best alternative use of an asset.

10. Externalities – 479 – The ways in which accepting a project affects the cash flows in other part of the company.

11. Initial Investment Outlay – 480 – the incremental cash flowsassociated with a project that will occur only at the start of the project's life.

12. Incremental Operating Cash Flows – 480 – The changes in day-to-day cash flows that result from the purchase of a capital

project and continue until the firm disposes of the asset.

13. Terminal Cash Flow – 481 – The net cash flow that occurs at the end of the life of the a project.

14. Payback Period – The length of time before the original cost of an investment is recovered from the expected cash flows.

15. Required Rate of Return – 494 -The discount rate (cost of funds) that the Incremental Rate of Return (IRR) must exceed for a project to be considered acceptable.

16. Types of Risk –(502-503)

a. Stand Alone Risk – a company's only asset risk

b. Corporate Risk – the stockholder's risk

c. Beta Risk – a project's risk that cannot be eliminated by diversification

d. Scernario Risk – an imaginary analysis of various scenarios for risk

e. Worst Case Scenario Risk – an analysis of the worst forecast values*

f. Best Case Scenario Risk – an analysis of the best forecast values

g. Base Case Scenario Risk – an analysis that is measured against a constant forecast value

h. Exchange Rate Risk – 507 – the uncertainty associated with the price of one currency versus the price of another currency

i. Political Risk – 508 – the risk associated with the political stability of the country in which the project is being executed.

ICA and HW 12

Answer these essay questions:

1. Why should sunk costs be eliminated from a capital budgeting analysis?

2. How is net working capital recovered at the end of a project's life?

31

3. How do types of risk differ?
4. How do companies evaluate risk?

Internet Resources for this lesson:

General Reference Material For All Content

http://www.askmrmovies.com

Risk
www.investopedia.com

Project Analysis

www.intaver.com/index-whitepapers.html

Tafero's Lesson Plans of Day - Finance - Capital Structure - Thirteen

Lesson 13 – Capital Structure and Dividend Policy Decisions

Reinvesting dividends is an effective wealth-builder

1. Capital Structure – 526 – The combination of debt and equity usedto finance a firm.
2. Target Capital Structure – 527 – The mix of debt preferred stockand common equity with which the company plans to finance its investments.
3. Business Risk – 528 – The risk associated with projections of a company's future returns on assets (educated guesses, often wrong) if the company uses no debt.
4. Business Risk Variables – 529
a. Sales Variability – (volume and price) – the more stable the unit sales (volume) and prices of a company's product, the lower its risk
b. Input Price Variability – labor, product cost variations are low-risk when stable and high-risk when unstable
c. Ability to Adjust Output Prices for Changes in Input Prices – the faster you can raise or lower your prices in relation to their input costs, the less risk you incur
d. Operating Leverage Risk – fixed assets do not change as rapidly as product changes, so there is more risk attached to them because of their lack of liquidity.
5. Financial Risk – 530 – The portion of stockholders risk over and above the basic business risk.
6. Financial Leverage – 530 – the extent to which fixed-income securities (debt and preferred stock) are used in a firm's capital structure.
7. Times Interest Earned (TIE) ration – 541 - a ratio that measures a firm's ability to meet it annual interest obligations.
8. Symmetric Information – 544 – The situation in which investors and managers have identical information.
9. Asymmetric Information – 544- The situation in which investors do not have the same information that managers have (not recommended).

10. Signal – 545 – An action taken by management that provides clues to investors about how management views the company's prospects (whether they buy or sell their stock options)

11. Reserve Borrowing Capacity – 545 – The ability to borrow money at a reasonable cost when investment opportunities arise.

12. Dividends – 547 – Distributions made to stockholders from the company's earnings.

13. Optimal Dividend Policy – 548 – The dividend policy that strikes a balance between currentdividends and future growth while maximizing the firm's stock price.

14. Information Content (signaling) Hypothesis - 549 – The theory that investors regard dividend changes as signals of management's earnings forecast (guesses).

15. Clientele Effect – 549 – The tendency of a company to attract the type of investor who likes its dividend policy.

16. Free Cash Flow Hypothesis – 549 – Companies that pay dividends from cash flows that canned be reinvested any other way.

17. Residual Dividend Policy – 550 – Dividends that are distributed after all other expenses are satisfied.

18. Stable, Predictable Dividends (not really that predictable) – 551 – Payment of a specific dollar dividend per share per year with periodic increases or decreases.

19. Extra Dividend – 552- A supplemental dividend paid to stockholders when the company does well.

20. Declaration Date – 553 – The date on which the company's board issues a statement declaring a dividend.

21. Holder of Record Date – 553 – The date on which the company opens the ownership books to determine who will receive the dividend.

22. Ex-Dividend Date – 553 – The date on which the right to the next dividend no longer accompanies a stock.

23. Payment Date – 553 – The date on which a company actually mails the dividend checks.

24. Dividend Reinvestment Plan – 553 – A plan that enables a stockholder to automatically reinvest dividends received back into the stock.

25. Stock Split – 556 – An action taken by the company to increase the number of shares outstanding. This means that an $50 stock becomes $25 but you now have two shares at $25.

26. Stock Dividend – 556- A dividend paid in the form of additional shares of stock.

ICA and HW 13

Answer these essay questions:

1. How can companies with relatively stable sales carry relatively high debt/assets ratios?
2. How would an increase in the personal income tax rate affect dividends?
3. How would a rise in interest rates affect dividends?
4. How would a decline in corporate investment opportunities affect dividends?

Internet Resources for this lesson:

General Reference Material For All Content

http://www.askmrmovies.com

Dividends
www.investopedia.com

Stock Splits

www.sec.gov/answers/stocksplit.htm

Tafero's Lesson Plans of Day - Finance - Working Capital - Fourteen

Lesson 14 – Working Capital Management

1. Working Capital Management – 574 – The management of short-term assets (investments) and liabilities (financing sources).
2. Working Capital – 574 – A company's investment in short-term assets (cash, stocks, inventory)
3. Net Working Capital – 574 – Current Assets minus CurrentLiabilities
4. Working Capital Policy – 574 – Decisions regarding target levels of each asset
5. Cash Conversion Cycle – 577 – The length of time from the payment for the purchase of raw materials to manufacture until thecollection of accounts.
6. Relaxed Current Asset Investment Policy *****-580 – policy that allows large amounts of cash and securities to be carried on the books; this policy resulted in many abuses during the global financial crisis.
7. Restricted Current Asset Investment Policy – 580 – this is the current policy in effect in almost all international companies presently. Holdings of receivables are minimized and excessive debt is not carried.
8. Moderate Current Asset Investment Policy – 580 – This is the first step beyond Restricted Current Asset Investment Policy and will take place once the aftereffects of the Global Financial Crisis have been remedied.
9. Permanent Current Assets – 581 – Current assets' balances that do not change due to seasonal or economic conditions.
10. Temporary Current Assets – 581 – Current Assets that fluctuate with seasonal or economic conditions. (this is by far the most common type of asset)
11. Short-Term Credit – 584 – Any liability originally scheduled for repayment within one year.
12. Accruals – 584 – Continually recurring short-

term liabilities such as wages and taxes.

13. Trade Credit – 584 – The credit created when one company buys on credit from another company.

14. Promissory Note – 585 – A document specifying the terms and conditions of a loan.

15. Line of Credit – 585 – An arrangement in which the bank agrees to lend up to a specified maximum amount of funds during a designated period.

16. Commercial Paper – 586 – Unsecured, short-term promissory notes issued by large, financially sound companies to raise funds.

17. Secured Loan – 586 – A loan backed by collateral.

18. Factoring – 586 – The outright sale of accounts receivable. ***** These assets sometimes turned out to be toxic or have overstated values and are now much more closely supervised by national governments.

19. Recourse – 586 – A situation in which the lender can seek payment from the borrowing company when the accounts receivable used to secure the loan are uncollectable ****** (this occurred in the real estate sector with banks holding uncollectable mortgages; too many of these types of loans also contributed to the Global Financial Crisis)

20. Discount Interest Loans – 589 – a loan in which the interest is paid first, such as in a mortgage. Only a small part of the principal is paid off while the interest is still being paid.

ICA and HW 14

Cash Management

Answer the following essay questions

1. How do we compute the cost of Short-Term Credit?
2. Discuss some of the advantages and disadvantages of Short-Term Financing
3. How should current assets be financed?
4. Discuss the cash conversion cycle.

Internet Resources for this lesson:

General Reference Material For All Content

http://www.askmrmovies.com

Cash Management

www.inc.com

Short-Term Financing
www.britannica.com/EBchecked/topic/.../short-term-financing

Tafero's Lesson Plans of Day - Finance - Managing Cash - Fifteen

Lesson 15 – Managing Cash and Marketable Securities

1. Transaction Balance - 590 – A cash balance necessary for day-to-day operations.
2. Precautionary Balance – 590 – A cash balance held in reserve for unforeseen fluctuations in cash flows.
3. Speculative Balance – 590 – A cash balance held to enable the company to take advantage of any bargain purchases that might arise.
4. Synchronized Cash Flows – 591- A situation in which cash inflows coincide with cash outflows creating low transaction balances.
5. Float – 591 – not cola and vanilla ice cream, but the difference between the balance shown in a company's checkbook and the balance on the bank records.
6. Disbursement Float – 591 – The value of the checks that have been written and disbursed, but have not yet cleared.
7. Collections Float – 591 – The amount of checks that have been received and deposited, but are not yet credited to the account.
8. Net Float – 591 – The difference between disbursement float andcollections float.
9. Marketable Securities – 593 – Securities that can be sold on short notice without loss of the principal or original investment.
10. Credit Policy – 594 – A set of decisions that includes a firm's credit standards, credit terms, methods used to collect credit accounts and credit monitoring procedures.
11. Credit Standards – 594 – Standards that indicate the minimum financial strength a customer must have to be granted credit.***** (most of these standards failed during the recent

Global Financial Crisis)

12. Terms of Credit – 595 – The payment conditions offered to credit customers.

13. Days Sales Outstanding – 595 – The average length of time required to collect accounts receivable.

14. Aging Schedule – 595 – A report showing how long accounts receivable have been outstanding.

15. Raw Materials – 600 – The inventories purchased from suppliers.

16. Work-In-Process – 600 – Inventory in various stages of completion.

17. Finished Goods – 600 – Inventory finished and ready for sale.

18. Carrying Costs – 600 – The cost of storing your inventory not sold.

19. Economic Ordering Quantity (EOQ) – 601 – The optimal quantity that should be ordered to minimize inventory costs.

20. Reorder Point – 605 – The level of inventory at which an order should be placed.

21. Investment Banker – 605 – An organization that underwrites and distributes new issues of securities.

22. Red-Line Method – 605 – An inventory control measure that indicates when you should buy more inventory.

23. Just-In-Time System – 605 – An economical, but chancy method of maintaining zero inventory.

24. Outsourcing – 605 – The practice of purchasing components of a product rather than making them inhouse.

ICA and HW 15

Loans will be more difficult to get after the Global Financial Crisis

Answer these essay questions:

1. Describe the cash conversion cycle.
2. Describe the three categories of inventories.
3. Discuss Aging schedules.
4. How can holding cash be an advantage?

Internet Resources for this lesson:

General Reference Material For All Content

http://www.askmrmovies.com

Credit
www.ftc.gov/bcp/menus/consumer/credit.shtm

Inventory Control

www.businesslink.gov.uk/bdotg/action/layer?topicId

Tafero's Lesson Plans of Day - Finance - Investment Concepts - Sixteen

Lesson 16 – Investment Concepts

Investment is a game with clear winners and losers

1. Investors – 624 – Individuals who purchase investments with savings in anticipation of stable growth.
2. Speculators – 624 – Individuals who take large risks in exchange for the possibility of large returns. Similar to gambling.
3. Income Securities – 625 – Investments, such as preferred stock and corporate bonds, that offer steady dividend or interest payments
4. Transaction Cost – 627 – The costs associated with trading securities usually in commission form.
5. Investment Portfolio – 627 – a combination of investment items designed to reduce risk for the client.
6. Asset Allocation – 627 – The proportion of funds invested in various categories of assets.
7. Broker – 629 – A middleman or agent who helps investors trade financial instruments such as stocks, bonds and derivatives (now much more strongly regulated after the Global Financial Crisis)
8. Brokerage Firm – 629 – a group of salesmen who make educated guesses about investments.
9. Market Order – 630 – An order to execute a transaction at the best price available.
10. Stop Order – 631 – An order that specifies the price at which a market order is initiated.
11. Limit Order – 631 – An order to buy or sell a stock at no worse than a specified price.
12. Day Order (DO) – 631 – An instruction to cancel an order if price conditions are not met by end of one day's business.
13. Good Til Cancelled (GTC) – 631 – An instruction to keep an

order active until the price limitations are met or until the investor cancels it.

14. Fill or Kill Order – 631 – An instruction to cancel an order if it is not executed immediately (the term immediately is relative, but generally means in a few minutes).

15. Street Name – 631 – A situation in which stock is registered to the brokerage firm instead of the individual investor. This can be a an additional risk for the investor.

16. Stock Symbol – 635 – The trading initials of a company used for transactions.

ICA and HW 16

The New York Stock Exchange is the most famous financial institution in the world

Answer the following essay questions:

1. How is investing in securities similar to gambling?
2. How does a balanced portfolio help to reduce risk to an investor?
3. How are some brokerage firms unethical in their recommendations?
4. How can the timing of a market order of even ten minutes have positive or negative repercussions to an investor?

Internet Resources for this lesson:

General Reference Material For All Content

http://www.askmrmovies.com

New York Stock Exchange
www.nyse.com/

Brokerage Firms
www.savings-secrets.com/

Tafero's Lesson Plans of Day - Finance - Computing Investment Returns - Seventeen

Lesson 17 – Computing Investment Returns

Investment does not necessarily mean an increase in your returns

1. Dollar Return – 639- = Income received + (Ending Value of an Investment – Beginning Value of an Investment) or INC + (P1 – P0).
2. Holding Period Return (HPR) – 640 – The return earned over the period of time that an investment is held.
3. Dividend Yield – 640 – The part of the total return associated with the dividends paid by the firm.
4. Capital Gain or Loss – 640 – A change in the market value of a security.
5. Simple Arithmetic Average Return – 641 – A technique forcomputing the average return on an investment that sums each return and divides the number of returns; does not include compounding.
6. Market Capitalization – 648 – The total market value of a company's stock which is computed by multiplying the number of shares outstanding by the market price per share.
7. Bull and Bear Markets – 650 – bull is a rising market, while bear is a falling market.
8. Buy and Hold Strategy – 651 – When investors purchase securities with the intention of holding them for a number of years.
9. Margin Trading – 651 – Incredibly, although greatly modified after the Great Depression of 1929, was still a major factor in the Global Financial Crisis. Additional modifications have been made to reduce the impact of this practice. It is the practice of borrowing from a broker a portion of the funds needed to purchase an investment.

10. Hypothecation Agreement – 651 – A contract that assigns securities as collateral for a margin loan.
11. Margin Call – 653 – A call from the broker to add more funds to a margined account.
12. Maintenance Margin – 653 – The lowest actual margin that the broker will permit margined investors to have at any time.
13. Broker Loan Rate – 652 – The rate charged by brokers to borrow funds for margin trading.
14. Sort Selling – 654 – A situation in which an investor borrows the stock of another investor and then sells it, but promises to replace the stock at a later date. (This is another risky practice).
15. Downticks and Upticks – 655 – The decrease or increase of a stock price from one trade to another. A small tick either way can make the difference of thousands of dollars in a large order.
16. Zero-Plus tick – 655 – A situation in which the price of the latest trade equals the price of the previous trade, but exceeds the price from one trade to another. (this is an assumption to the uptick)
17. Shorting Against the Box – 655 – When an investor short sells a stock that he or she also owns. This is a form of betting against yourself.

ICA and HW 17

Investing is a gambling game best left to professionals

Answer the following essay questions:

1. Why is past performance of a stock no guarantee that it will continue to rise?
2. Why is market capitalization one of the most important variables for you to consider beforeinvesting in a stock?

3. How can margin buying be a dangerous practice?
4. Why is the buy and hold strategy not a foolproof method of investing?

Internet Resources for this lesson:

General Reference Material For All Content

http://www.askmrmovies.com

Market Capitalization
www.investorwords.com/2969/market_capitalization.html

Margin Buying
www.investopedia.com

Lesson 18 – Security Valuation and Selection

A Columbia University student actually did an experiment with a monkey throwing five darts at stocks that outperformed over 70% of all brokerage house selections for the year 2001.

(source: Business Week)

1. Fundamental Analysis – 669 – The practice of actually looking at published financial statements of a company before investing.
2. Technical Analysis – 669 – The practice of betting on stocks loosely based on various questionable theories of supply and demand.
3. Business Cycle – 670 - the movement in aggregate economic activity as measured by the gross domestic product.
4. Gross Domestic Product – 670 – A measure of all goods and services produced in the economy during a specific time period.
5. Recession – 671- Two consecutive quarters of economic contraction or decline in the GDP
6. Leading Economic Indicators – 672 – Economic measures that tend to move prior to movements in the business cycle.
7. Lagging Economic Indicators – 672 – Economic measures that tend to move after movements in the business cycle.
8. Monetary Policy – 675 – The means by which a country influences economic conditions by managing its money supply.
9. Fiscal Policy – 675 – Government spending which is primarily supported by the government's ability to tax individuals and businesses.
10. Deficit Spending – 675 – Spending that occurs when the government spends more funds than it collects in taxes.
11. Industry Life Cycle – 677 – The various phases of an industry with respect to its growth in sales and competition variables.
12. P.E Ratio – 684 – A ration computed by dividing the current market price per share, P0, by the earnings per share EPS0.
13. Bar Chart – 688 – A graph that indicates the high, low, and closing price movements for a stock during a specified period.

14. Trendline – 688 – A line that indicates the direction of the stock price movement. The longer the time period involved for the line direction, the better your chances that the stock will continue in that direction.

15. Dow Theory – 689 – Theory used to predict price movements base on the Dow Jones Industrial and Transportation averages (this theory has been proven to be highly unreliable).

16. Moving Average – 689 – Stock price averages for a fixed period of time. Absolutely no indicator or predictor of prices for even one day.

17. Growth Stocks – 692 – Stocks of companies that have many positive sales and earnings figures that outperform industry averages.

18. Value Stocks – 693 – Stocks of companies that are mispriced; especially those that are undervalued using the market capitalization computations.

ICA and HW 18

Finding Highly Profitable Stocks in the Post-GFC World

Answer the following essay questions:

1. Why is investing in a Bear Market far more difficult than investing in a Bull Market?
2. Why are fundamental analysts safer to use than technical analysts for investing?
3. Why is Market Capitalization still one of the most important factors for investing?
4. Why are Technical theories still useful for some investing?

Internet Resources for this lesson:

General Reference Material For All Content

http://www.askmrmovies.com

Fundamental Investment

www.investopedia.com/university/fundamentalanalysis/

Technical Investment
www.investmentweek.co.uk/tag/technical

Part Two of Intermediate Business Courses – Bernanke Macroeconomics

Arthur H Tafero

Tafero's Lesson Plans of Day - Bernanke Macroeconomics - Thinking Like an Economist - One

Lesson 1- Thinking as an Economist

1. The Scarcity Principle 3 – if someone has more, someone else has less
2. The Cost-Benefit Principle 3 – no action should be taken unlessthe benefit is at least equal to the cost
3. Incentive Principle 3 – Prediction of behavior is primarily based on knowing incentives
4. Measurement of Cost 3 – should be in absolute dollar amounts and not in proportions
5. Economics – 4 – the study of how people make choices under conditions of scarcity and the results of those choices on society
6. Economic Surplus – 6 – The benefit of taking an action minus its cost
7. Opportunity Cost – 7 – The value that may be gained by taking an action minus its cost
8. Sunk Cost – 11 – A cost that is beyond recovery when a decision must be made
9. Marginal Cost -12 – the cost of carrying out one additional activity that is added to the total cost
10. Marginal Benefit – 12 – the increase in total benefits that result from carrying out an additional activity
11. Average Cost – 12 – the total cost of undertaking X units of an activity divided by X
12. Average Benefit – 12 – the total benefit of undertaking X units

ofan activity divided by X
13. Normative Economic Principle 15 – how people should behave statistically
14. Positive Economic Principle 15 – one that predicts how people will behave
15. Microeconomics – 15 – the study of individual choice under scarcity and the behavior of prices and quantities in individual markets
16. Macroeconomics – 15 – the study of the performance of national economies and government policies that try to improve performance

ICA and HW 1

Answer the following essay questions

1. Why should we measure cost or benefit in absolute dollars instead of a propotion?
2. Why should we always be aware of implicit costs?
3. Describe Cost-Benefit Analysis.
4. Discuss the Scarcity Principle.

Internet Resources for this lesson

General Reference
http://www.askmrmovies.com

Cost-Benefit Analysis

The Scarcity Principle

Tafero's Lesson Plans of Day - Bernanke Macroeconomics - Spending, Income and GDP - Two

Lesson 2 – Spending, Income and GDP

1. Gross Domestic Product 38 – (GDP) – the market value of the final goods and services provided in a country during a given period.

2. Final Goods or Services – 41 – Goods or services consumed by the ultimate user

3. Intermediate Goods or Services – 41 – Goods or services used up in the production of final goods and services.

4. Capital Good – 42 – a long-lived good that is used in the production of other goods and services. Goods may be actual physical items or they may be services provided by vendors that do not require and physical items.

5. Value Added – 43 – market value of its product or service minus the cost of inputs purchased from other firms. A good example ofvalue added strategy that works in the modern market is that of Walmart, which offers moderate quality at a low price, thereby affording the consumer added value.

6. Consumption – 46 – spending by households on goods and services such as food, clothing, and entertainment

7. Investment – 46 – spending by companies on final goods and services in the capital goods sector.

8. Government Purchases – purchases by federal, state and local governments of final goods and services.

9. Net exports -47 48 – exports minus imports

10. GDP = Consumption + Investment + Government Purchases +Net Exports or Y= C+I+G+NX

11. Real GDP – 51 – a measure of GDP in which the quantities produced are valued at the prices of a base year rather than at current prices

12. Nominal GDP – 51 – a measure of GDP in which the quantities produced are valued at current year prices.

ICA and HW 2
Answer these essay questions

1. Discuss the difference between nominal and real GDP.
2. How do we calculate the formula for GDP?
3. Discuss the differences between final goods and services and intermediate goods and services.
4. What would be some types of government purchases?

Internet Resources for this lesson

General Reference
http://www.askmrmovies.com

GDP

Final Goods versus Intermediate Goods

Tafero's Lesson Plans of Day - Bernanke Macroeconomics - Inflation and Price Level - Three

Lesson 3 – Inflation and Price Levels

1. Consumer Price Index (CPI) – 66 – measures the cost of a standard basket of goods for a specified period over and above the cost of the same items from the immediate previous specified period

2. Price Index – 68 – an average price of a given class of goods or services

3. Rate of Inflation – 68 – the annual percentage rate of change in the price levels of goods and services

4. Deflation – 69 – a rarely seen phenomena of the price levels going down.

5. Nominal Quantity – 70 – a quantity that is measured in terms of its current dollar value. Ex: job earnings are 30K in 2011, then 31K in 2012

6. Real Quantity – 70 – a quantity that is measured in physical terms related to the CPI. Ex: if CPI went up 10% in 2012, then your real earnings for 2012 were only 28K

7. Delating – 70 – the process of dividing a nominal quantity by aprice index such as the CPI to express the quantity in real terms.

8. Real Wage – 71 – wages paid to workers measured in purchasing power or real terms.

9. Indexing – 72 – the practice of increasing a nominal quantity each period by an amount equal to the percentage increase of the CPI.

10. Price Level – 76 – a measure of the overall level of prices at a particular point in time as measured by a price index such as the CPI

11. Relative Price – 76 – The price of a specific good or service in comparison to the prices of other goods and services.

12. Hyperinflation – 82 – A situation in which the inflation rate is extremely high.

13. Real Interest Rates – 84 – the annual percentage increase in the purchasing power of a financial asset. Ex house worth

100,000 in 2011 and now 102,000 after inflation factored

14. Nominal Interest Rate -84 – the annual percentage increase in the nominal increase in the nominal value of a financial asset Ex house worth 100,000 in 2011 now worth 105,000 on the market, but only worth 102,000 in real dollars.

15. Inflation-Protected Bonds – 86 – bonds that pay a nominal interest rate each year equal to a fixed rated plus the actual rate of inflation that year.

16. Fisher Effect – 87 – interest is high when inflation is high and low when inflation is low.

ICA and HW 3
Answer the following essay questions

1. Discuss the comparison of nominal and real interest rates
2. Discuss the relationship of price levels to relative price
3. Discuss the comparison of nominal wages to real wages.
4. Discuss the relationship of the price index to inflation

Internet Resources for this lesson

General Reference
http://www.askmrmovies.com

Nominal and Real Wages

Consumer Price Index

Tafero's Lesson Plans of Day - Bernanke Macroeconomics - Wages and Unemployment - Four

Lesson 4 – Wages and Unemployment

1. Real Wage Trend – 94
a. In the 20th century, all industrialized countries enjoyed an increase in real wages
b. Since the 1970s, real wage increases have slowed
c. The last 20 years have brought a pronounced increase in wage inequality in the US and many other industrialized nations.

2. Unemployment Trends – 95
a. In the US and many other industrialized countries the nominalnumber of people with jobs has grown substantially in the last 20 years.
b. At the same time, Western European countries have had high rates of unemployment for the same time period (this is connected to the earlier pensions and retirement systems of these countries)
3. Diminishing Returns to Labor – 96 – if the amount of capital and other inputs are constant, then the greater the quantity of labor already employed, the less additional worker adds to production
4. The Demand Curve for Labor – 98 – the demand curve for labor is downward-sloping. The higher the wage, the fewer workers employers will hire.
5. The Supply of Labor – 102 – the labor supply curve is upward sloping because the higher the wage, the more people that are willing to work
6. Worker Mobility – 108 – the movement of workers between jobs, companies and industries.
7. Skill-Based Technological Change – 109 – technological change that affects the marginal products of higher-skilled workers differently from those of lower-skilled workers.
8. Labor Force – 111 – the total number of employed and unemployed people in the economy.
9. Unemployment Rate – 111 – the number of unemployed

people divided by the labor force

10. Participation Rate – 111 – the percentage of the working-age population in the labor force.

11. Structural Unemployment – 115 – long-term and chronic unemployment regardless of the condition of the economy.

12. Cyclical Unemployment – 116 – the extra unemployment that occurs during periods of recession.

ICA and HW 4

Answer the following essay questions

1. Compare structural unemployment to cyclical unemployment.

2. Compare the supply and demand for labor in terms of curves.

3. Describe the difference between participation rates and unemployment rates.

4. Discuss the current unemployment trends and real wages trends in your country.

Internet Resources for this lesson

General Reference

http://www.askmrmovies.com

Unemployment Trends

Real Wage Trends

Tafero's Lesson Plans of Day - Bernanke Macroeconomics - Economic Growth and Savings - Five

Lesson 5 – Economic Growth and Savings

1. The value of a currency is roughly equal to the individual output percentage of a person in one country that is compared to the person of another country. Example the output of the average American is about six and a half times greater than the output of an average Chinese. Consequently, the value of six and a half Chinese dollars (RMB) is only equal to about one US dollar.

2. Average Labor Productivity – 136 – output per employed worker

3. Compound Interest – 133 – the payment of interest not only on the original deposit, but on all other interest as well.

4. Human Capital – 239 – an amalgam of factors such as education, training, experience, intelligence, energy, work habits, trustworthiness, initiative, and others that affect the value of worker's marginal product.

5. Diminishing Returns to Capital – 141 – If the amount of labor and other inputs are constant, then the greater the amount of capital already in use, the less an additional unit of capital adds to production.

6. Entrepreneurs – 144 – people who create new economic enterprises

7. Savings – 163 – current income minus spending on current needs

8. Saving rate – 163 – saving divided by income

9. Wealth – 163 – the value of assets minus liabilities

10. Assets – 163 – anything of value that one owns

11. Liabilities – 163 – the debts one owes

12. Balance Sheet – 163 – a list of economic units of assets and liabilities

13. Flow – 164 – a measure that is defined per unit of time

14. Stock – 164 – a measure that is defined at a point in time

15. Capital Gains – 165– increases in the value of existing assets

16. Capital Losses – 165 – decreases in the values of existing assets

ICA and HW 5
Answer the following essay questions

1. Discuss human capital.
2. Discuss diminishing returns to capital
3. Discuss the effects of compound interest in both terms of savings and debt
4. Discuss the issue of productivity in relation to other countries

Internet Resources for this lesson

General Reference
http://www.askmrmovies.com

Compound Interest

Productivity

Tafero's Lesson Plans of Day - Bernanke Macroeconomics - National Savings, Investment and Capital - Six

Lesson 6 – National Savings, Investment and Capital

1. National Saving – 168 – the saving of the entire economy, equal to the GDP less consumption expenditures and government purchases of goods and services.
2. Transfer Payments – 169- payments the government makes to the public for which it receives no current goods or services
3. Private Saving – 169 - the saving of the private sector of the economy is equal to the after-tax income of the private sector minus consumption expenditures. This is an extremely important part of a country's ability to balance its budget; just as saving as an average family is important for that family to make economic progress.
4. Public Saving – 169 – the saving of the government sector is equal to net tax payments minus government purchases. This implies that the government will be prudent when spending tax dollars.
5. Government Budget Surplus – 170 – the excess of government tax collections over government spending. Rather than just letting this money lie in banks, it is sometimes better to reinvest the savings in more aggressive projects that will save money in thefuture. These might include capital expenditures for improving infrastructure or transportation, which will add more tax dollars to the tax base.
6. Government Budget Deficit – 170 – the excess of government spending over tax collections. This should always be kept to a minimum as interest paid on this amount does not serve any positive purpose in the economy.
7. Life-cycle savings – 173 – saving to meet long-term objectives such as retirement or a home
8. Precautionary saving – 173 – saving for protection against unexpected setbacks such as loss of a job or medical problems
9. Bequest saving – 173 – saving done for the purpose of leaving an inheritance

10. Crowding out – 184 – the tendency of increased government deficits to reduce investment spending.

ICA and HW 6

Answer the following essay questions

1. Discuss national saving. How does national saving affect the national economy?
2. Compare private and public saving
3. Compare Government surpluses and deficits and the effects they have on an economy.
4. Discuss the concept of crowding out. How can this negatively impact a country's economy?

Internet Resources for this lesson

General Reference
http://www.askmrmovies.com

Crowding Out

Government Deficit Repercussions

Tafero's Lesson Plans of Day - Bernanke Macroeconomics - The Financial System, Money, and Prices - Seven

Lesson 7 – The Financial System, Money and Prices

1. Financial Intermediaries 192 – firms that extend credit to borrowers using funds raised from savers.
2. Bond 194 – a legal promise to repay a debt, usually including both the principal amount and regular interest payments.
3. Principal Amount 194 – the amount originally lent
4. Maturation Date 194 – the date at which the principal will be repaid
5. Coupon Payments 194 – regular interest payments made to the bondholder
6. Coupon Rate 194 – the interest rate promised when a bond is issued: the annual coupon payments are equal to the coupon rate times the principal amount of the bond.
7. Stock (equity) 196 – a claim to partial ownership of a firm
8. Dividend 196 – a regular payment received by stockholders for each share that they own
9. Risk premium 198 – the rate of return that financial investors require to hold risky assets minus the rate of return on safe assets
10. Diversification 199 – the practice of spreading one's wealth over a variety of different financial investments to reduce overall risk
11. Mutual Fund 201 –a financial intermediary that sells shares in itself to the public, then uses the funds raised to buy a wide variety of financial assets (usually stock)
12. Money 201 – any asset that can be used in making purchases
13. Medium of exchange 202 – an asset used in purchasing goods and services
14. Barter 202 – the direct trade of goods or services for other goods or services
15. Unit of Account 202 – a basic measure of economic value
16. Store of Value 202 – an asset that serves as a means of holding wealth

17. M1 203 – sum of currency outstanding and balances held in checking accounts
18. M2 203 – all the assets in M1 plus some additional assets that are usable in making payments but at greater cost or inconvenience than currency or checks
19. Reserve-deposit ratio 206 – bank reserves divided by depositors
20. Fractional-reserve banking system 206 – a banking system in which bank reserves are less that deposits so that the reserve-deposit ratio is less than 100 percent
21. Federal Reserve System (FED) 210 – the central bank of the United States
22. Open-Market Purchase 211 – the purchase of government bonds from the public by the FED for the purpose of increasing the supply of bank reserves and the money supply
23. Open-Market Sale 211 – the sale by the FED of government bonds to the public for the purpose of reducing bank reserves and the money supply
24. Open-Market Operations 211 – open market purchases and open-market sales
25. Velocity 212 – the speed at which money changes hands in transactions involving final goods and services

ICA and HW 7

Answer the following essays

1. Discuss the Open Market.
2. Discuss M1 and M2 calculations.
3. Discuss Diversification.
4. Discuss Financial Intermediaries.

Internet Resources for this lesson

General Reference
http://www.askmrmovies.com

Diversification

Financial Intermediaries

Tafero's Lesson Plans of Day - Bernanke Macroeconomics - Short-Term Economic Fluctuations - Eight

Lesson 8 – Short-Term Economic Fluctuations

1. Recession 225 – a period in which the economy is growing at a rate significantly below normal. Recessions are considered an improvement over depressions, but a step back from expansion.
2. Depression 225 – a particularly severe or protracted recession. The length of a depression can severely affect a national economy.
3. Peak 226 – the beginning of a recession; the high point prior to a downturn
4. Trough 226 – at the end of a recession; the low point of economic activity prior to a recovery
5. Expansion 227 – a period in which the economy is growing at a rate significantly above normal. This percentage cannot be sustained for an extended number of years without causing some collateral damage.
6. Boom 227 – a particularly strong and protracted expansion
7. Potential Output Y 231 – the maximum sustainable amount of output (real GDP) that an economy can produce
8. Output Gap Y 232 – the difference between the economy's actual output and its potential output as a point in time
9. Recessionary Gap 232 – a negative output gap, which occurs when potential output exceeds actual output. This is a naturaloccurrence, since populations tend to spend less during recessions.
10. Expansionary Gap 232 – a positive output gap, which occurs when actual output is higher than potential output. This is a naturaloccurrence, since populations most often spend more during expansionary periods.
11. Natural Rate of Unemployment 233 – the part of the total unemployment rate that is attributable to frictional and structural unemployment. This figure must be added to the underemployment figures to get a more realistic view of the true rate of unemployment in any country.
12. Okun's Law 295 – each extra percentage point of cyclical

unemployment is associated with about a 2 percentage point increase in the output gap.

ICA and HW 8

Answer the following essays:

1. Discuss Okun's Law.
2. Discuss Output, Recessionary, and Expansionary Gaps.
3. Discuss the difference between recessions and depressions.
4. Discuss the natural rate of unemployment.

Internet Resources for this lesson

General Reference
http://www.askmrmovies.com

Recession and Depression

Natural Rate of Unemployment

Lesson Nine – Midterm Exam

Tafero's Lesson Plans of Day - Bernanke Macroeconomics - Simulating Economies – Lesson Ten

Lesson 10 – Simulation for National Economies

1. Each student will be assigned (randomly) a country. Each country will have a particular financial crisis that will have to be solved by various economic changes in policy. Some of the crises will be based on real historical occurrences and others will be purely fictional. The student will make recommendations to the leaders of each country to adjust various economic factors such as interest rates and inflationary controls. Additional problems could be one-time catastrophic occurrences that devastate current economies. Massive unemployment, overwhelming national debt, wars, massive disease, earthquakes, floods, recessions, depressions, and other negatively impacting events will be potentially applied to each country. The instructor may opt to put economic teams together for this simulation or have each student be completely alone in their simulation.

2. Variables to be considered by the individual or team:

a. Interest rates – lower rates = easier access to loans, higher rates lowers access

b. Inflation – low inflation may be a sign of stagnation, high inflation, a sign of an overheated economy or one that is broken down.

c. Unemployment – low unemployment generally indicates a healthy economy, while high unemployment is usually debilitating to an economy.

d. Political stability – Unstable governments tend to have unstable economies

e. Currency value – strong currencies must be balanced with diversification

f. National debt – should be kept to a minimum until a surplus can be achieved

g. Wars – usually detrimental to an economy

h. Epidemics – detrimental to all levels of the economy

i. Earthquakes – can be devastating to an economy (Japan)

j. Floods – must be controlled like India and China to lower effect on economies
k. Recessions – natural cycle in business
l. Depressions – an abnormal occurrence in the natural cycle of business
m. Excessive Pensions or Social Services – constant drain on healthy economies
n. Excessive Military Spending – constant drain on healthy economies

3. Students or teams will have one week to come up with solutions for the situational problem of each country.
4. The instructor will evaluate the solutions of the student or the team based on a reasonable application of macroeconomic principles applied to the situation.

ICA and HW 10

Answer the following essays:

1. How would you change interest rates to curb inflation?
2. How would you reduce national debt (any country)?
3. How would you correct excessive pensions and social services?
4. How would you correct excessive military spending?

Internet Resources for this lesson

General Reference
http://www.askmrmovies.com

Reducing National Debt

Reducing Military Spending

Tafero's Lesson Plans of Day - Bernanke Macroeconomics - Spending - Eleven

Lesson 11 – Spending and Output in the Short Run

1. Menu costs 246 – the cost of changing prices
2. Planned Aggregate Expenditure 247 – total planned spending on final goods and services
3. Consumption function 250 – the relationship betweenconsumption spending and its determinants such as disposable income
4. Autonomous consumption 250 – consumption spending that is not related to the level of disposable income
5. Wealth Effect 250 – the tendency of changes in asset prices to affect households' wealth and thus their consumption spending
6. Marginal propensity to consume 251 – the amount by whichconsumption rises when disposable income rises by \$1
7. Autonomous expenditure 253 – the portion of planned aggregateexpenditure that is independent of output
8. Induced expenditure 254 – the portion of planned aggregateexpenditure that depends on output Y.
9. Expenditure Line 254 – a line showing the relationship between planned aggregate expenditure and output
10. Short-run equilibrium output 255 – the level of output at which Y equals planned aggregate expenditure (PAE); short-run equilibrium output is the level of output that prevails during the period in which prices are predetermined
11. Income-Expenditure Multiplier 262 – the effect of a one-unit increase in autonomous expenditure on short-run equilibrium output
12. Stabilization policies 263 – government policies that are used to affect planned aggregate expenditure, with the objective of eliminating output gaps
13. Expansionary policies 263 – government policy actions designed to increase planned spending and output
14. Contraction policies 263 – government policy actions designed to reduce planned spending and output.

15. Automatic stabilizers 270 – provisions in the law that imply automatic increases in government spending or decreases in taxes when real output declines

ICA and HW 11

Answer the following essay questions

1. Discuss automatic stabilizers.
2. Discuss contraction, expansion and stabilization policies.
3. Discuss the income-expenditure multiplier.
4. Discuss the expenditure line,
induced expenditure and autonomous expenditures.

Internet Resources for this lesson

General Reference
http://www.askmrmovies.com

Economic Automatic Stabilizers

Income-Expenditure Multiplier

Tafero's Lesson Plans of Day - Bernanke Macroeconomics - Stabilizing an Economy - Twelve

Lesson 12 – Stabilizing the Economy and the Role of the FED

1. Federal Reserve System 286 – The Central Bank of the United States; also known as the FED
2. Board of Governors 287 – The leadership of the FED, consisting of seven governors appointed by the president to staggered 14 year terms.
3. Federal Open Market Committee (FOMC)-287 –
The committeethat makes decisions concerning monetary policy.
4. Banking Panic 288 – A situation in which news or rumors of the imminent bankruptcy of one or more banks leads bank depositors to rush to withdraw their funds. (Now all funds up to $100,000 apiece are insured by the FDIC; which means it is a good idea to have multiple bank accounts at that amount at many different banks)
5. Deposit Insurance 290 – a system under which the government guarantees that depositors will not lose their funds.
6. Federal Funds Rate 291 – the interest rate that commercial bankscharge each other for very short-term loans.
7. Monetary Policy Rule 301 – describes how a central bank takes action in response to changes in the state of the economy.
8. Target inflation rate 301 – the FED's long-run goal for inflation
9. Target real-interest rate 301 – the FED's long-run goal for the real interest rate
10. Portfolio Allocation Decision 304 – the decision about the forms in which to hold one's wealth
11. Demand for Money 304 – the amount of wealth an individual chooses to hold in the form of money.
12. Money Demand Curve 305 – Shows the relationship between the aggregate quantity of money demanded M and the nominal business rate, i.
13. Discount Window Lending 312 – the lending of reserves by the Federal Reserve to commercial banks.
14. Discount Rates (primary credit rate) 312 – the interest rate that the FED charges commercial banks to borrow reserves.

15. Reserve Requirements 313 – the minimum values set by the FED for ratios of bank deposits that commercial banks are allowed to maintain.

ICA and HW 12
Answer the following essay questions

1. Discuss the Money Demand Curve.
2. Discuss the importance of Deposit Insurance (FDIC).
3. Discuss the complexity of Portfolio Allocation Decisions.
4. Discuss the Federal Open Market Committee.

Internet Resources for this lesson

General Reference
http://www.askmrmovies.com

Money Demand Curve

Federal Open Market Committee

Tafero's Lesson Plans of Day - Bernanke Macroeconomics - Aggregate Supply and Demand and Macroeconomic Policy - Thirteen

Lesson 13 – Aggregate Demand and Supply

1. Long-Run Aggregate Supply (LRAS) Line 324 – a vertical line showing the economy's potential output (Y).
2. Exogenous Changes in Spending 327 – changes in planned spending that are not caused by changes in output or the realinterest rate
3. Tightening Monetary Policy 329 – a situation where the FED lowers its long-run target for the inflation rate
4. Easing Monetary Policy 329 – a situation where the FED raises its long-run target for the inflation rate.
5. Aggregate Supply Curve (ASC) 331 - shows the relationship between short-run equilibrium output Y and and inflation.
6. Inflation Shock -336 – a sudden change in the normal behavior of inflation
7. Long-run equilibrium – 337 – situation where actual input is equal to potential output and actual inflation equals expected inflation and the FED's inflation target.
8. Short-run equilibrium – 337 – situation where there is either an expansionary gap or a recessionary gap.
9. Aggregate Supply Shock – 346 – either an inflation shock or a shock to potential output.

ICA and HW 13
Answer the following essay questions

1. Discuss the Long-Run Aggregate Supply
2. Compare Tightening Monetary Policy to Easing Monetary Policy.
3. Discuss the Aggregate Supply Curve.
4. Compare Long-Run Equilibrium with Short-Run Equilibrium

Internet Resources for this lesson

General Reference

Long-Run Aggregate Supply

Aggregate Supply Curve

Lesson 14 – Macroeconomic Policy

1. Disinflation 357 – a substantial reduction in the rate of inflation
2. Accommodating Policy 359 – a policy that allows the effects of a shock to occur
3. Anchored Inflationary Expectations 363 – when people's expectations of future inflation do not change even if inflation is temporary
4. Core Rate of Inflation 365 – the rate of increase of all prices except energy and food
5. Credibility of Monetary Policy 366 – the degree to which the public believes the central bank's promises to keep inflation low, even if doing so may impose short-run economic costs.
6. Central Bank Independence 367 – when central bankers are insulated from short-term political considerations and are allowed to take a long-term view of the economy

7. Supply-Side Policy 372 – A policy that affects potential output
8. Marginal Tax Rate 373 – the amount by which taxes rise when before-tax income rises by one dollar
9. Average Tax Rate 373 – total taxes divided by total before-tax income
10. Inside Lag 378 – the delay between the date a policy change is needed and the actual date it is implemented
11. Outside Lag 379 – the delay between the date a policy change is implemented and the dateby which most of its effects on the economy have occurred

ICA and HW 14

Answer the following essays

1. Discuss the difference between an Inside Lag and an Outside in macroeconomic policy.
2. Discuss the difference between a Marginal Tax Rate and an Average Tax Rate.
3. Discuss the importance of Central Bank Independence.
4. Discuss the Core Rate of Inflation.

Internet Resources for this lesson

General Reference

http://www.askmrmovies.com

Core Rate of Inflation

Inside Lag and Outside Lag in Microeconomics